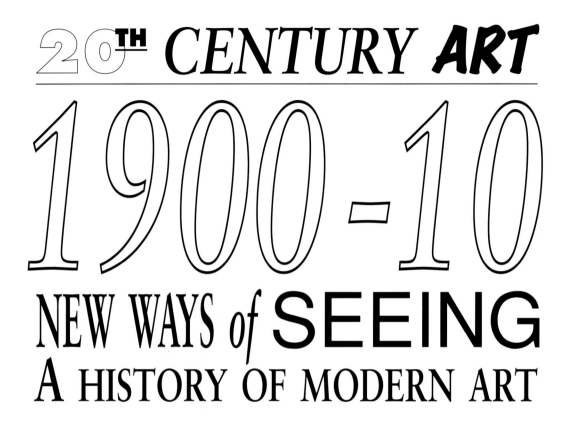

20TH CENTURY ART

1900-10

NEW WAYS of SEEING

A HISTORY OF MODERN ART

20TH CENTURY ART – 1900-10
was produced by

David West ☖ **Children's Books**

7 Princeton Court
55 Felsham Road
London SW15 1AZ

Picture Research: Brooks Krikler Research
Picture Editor: Carlotta Cooper

First published in Great Britain in 2000 by
Heinemann Library, Halley Court, Jordan Hill,
Oxford OX2 8EJ, a division of Reed Educational and
Professional Publishing Limited.

OXFORD MELBOURNE AUCKLAND
JOHANNESBURG BLANTYRE GABORONE
IBADAN PORTSMOUTH (NH) USA CHICAGO

04 03 02 01 00
10 9 8 7 6 5 4 3 2 1

ISBN 0 431 11600 8 (HB)
ISBN 0 431 11607 5 (PB)

British Library Cataloguing in Publication Data

Gaff, Jackie
1900 - 1910 New ways of seeing. - (Twentieth
century art)
1. Art, Modern - 20th century - Juvenile literature
I. Title
709' .041

Printed and bound in Italy

PHOTO CREDITS :
Abbreviations: t-top, m-middle, b-bottom, r-right, l-
left, c-centre.

Front cover & page 17b - Tate Publishing © ADAGP,
Paris & DACS, London, 2000. 3, 16t & 16 both -
Mary Evans Picture Library. 4, 9t, 12l, 13r, 14bl, 17t,
18l, 19b, 20b, 20b, 21l, 22l, 24t, 25 & 28t - AKG
London. 5t, 6 Both, 7t, 8, 9br, 10 both, 11t, 13l, 14t
& br, 15, 21r, 22r, 28b & 29t - Bridgeman Art Library.
5b - Bridgeman Art Library/Lauros-Giraudon. 12r -
J. Lathion ©Munch Museum/munch-ellingsen Group,
BONO, Oslo, DACS, London 2000. 19t - Bridgeman
Art Library © Succession H Matisse/DACS 2000. 20t -
AKG London © DACS 2000. 23 MOMA © Succession
Picasso/DACS 2000. 24b - Bridgeman Art
Library/Roger Violett, Paris. 26b - Bridgeman Art
Library © ADAGP, Paris & DACS, London 2000. 27 -
AKG London © ADAGP, Paris & DACS, London
2000. 29b - Bridgeman Art Library © ADAGP, Paris &
DACS, London 2000.

*The dates in brackets after a person's name
give the years that he or she lived.
The date that follows a painting's title and the
artist's name, gives the year it was painted.
'C.' stands for circa, meaning about or
approximately.*

*An explanation of difficult words can be
found in the glossary on page 30.*

20TH CENTURY ART
1900 - 10
NEW WAYS of SEEING
A HISTORY OF MODERN ART

Jackie Gaff

Heinemann
LIBRARY

CONTENTS

NEW LOOK CENTURY
5
MONET & IMPRESSIONISM
6
SEURAT & POINTILLISM
8
VAN GOGH & GAUGUIN
10
MUNCH & EXPRESSIONISM
12
SYMBOLISM
14
FAUVISM
16
MATISSE, KING OF COLOUR
18
NORTHERN EXPRESSIONISM
20
PICASSO'S *LES DEMOISELLES D'AVIGNON*
22
PAUL CEZANNE
24
CUBISM
26
CONSTANTIN BRANCUSI
28
GLOSSARY & TIMELINE
30
INDEX
32

YOUNG GENIUS
Spanish-born Pablo Picasso (1881–1973) was the most famous artist of the 20th century and, many believe, the greatest. He was 19, and few people outside his homeland had ever heard of him, when he visited Paris for the first time in 1900 – to see one of his paintings, which had been chosen for the Spanish pavilion at the Paris World's Fair.

NEW LOOK CENTURY

In the first decade of the 20th century Western art changed more than it had in the previous 500 years. Avant-garde painters abandoned naturalistic colour and perspective, and stopped painting the world as it appears to our eyes. What artists saw became less important than expressing their personal inner vision.

Most of these new ideas were born in France, whose capital, Paris, had long been the nerve centre of Western art. The story of modern art began there in the 19th century, when a group of young painters took the first steps in overthrowing 500 years of tradition. We now call this group the Impressionists, and their paintings are among the world's best loved. But back in 1874 when the term was coined, it was the horrified response of an art critic to the radical new style of Frenchman Claude Monet (1840–1926).

ART CAPITAL
Millions of people visited the Paris World's Fair in 1900, and thousands of paintings and sculptures from all around the world were shown in specially constructed new art galleries.

MODERN ART
As the bright young things of their day, Monet and the Impressionists were fascinated by modern technology – and the 19th century's biggest symbol of progress and speed was the steam engine!

LA GARE SAINT-LAZARE, *Claude Monet, 1877*

MONET & IMPRESSIONISM

The accepted painting style of Monet's day was an immaculately finished, almost photographic depiction of reality, which demanded a level of technical skill that took years of training to achieve. Artists worked indoors in their studios, even when painting landscapes, and a single work could take months to complete. The traditional subjects of art were weighty, and included religious and mythological scenes, and historical events.

PHOTO-REALITY
The invention of photography in the 1820s was to free artists from the duty of the exact depiction of reality. Painters were also inspired by the way snapshots could freeze a passing moment in time.

6

A MODERN WAY OF LIFE

The Impressionists, however, wanted to portray the bustling new society that had grown up outside their studios. Influenced by discoveries in optics, the science of light, they wanted to capture the way our eyes perceive the flickering, fleeting effects of natural light. To do this they had to work rapidly, using quick, rough brushstrokes. Their paintings looked sketchy and unfinished as a result, and this was what seemed so shocking to 19th-century eyes.

COLOUR THEORIES

Scientists had discovered that the brightness of a colour depends on the colours beside it. The vibrancy of Impressionist style came from using complementaries – the complementary of red is green, of yellow is purple, and of blue is orange.

Red, yellow and blue are primary colours.

AN INTERNATIONAL MOVEMENT
Impressionism had a huge impact worldwide. In the 1880s, Australians such as Arthur Streeton (1867–1943) and Tom Roberts (1856–1931) began using Impressionist techniques to portray the distinctive colours of the Australian landscape.

THE WALK (ARGENTEUIL)
CLAUDE MONET, *c.* 1872–75

Monet and the Impressionists often worked outdoors, painting snapshot-like images of modern Parisians enjoying weekends in the country – brought within easy reach of the city by the new railways. The Impressionists were fascinated by the play of natural light as it flickers off the surface of things, and their pictures seem to vibrate with colour. Painting outdoors was made possible by the invention of portable metal paint tubes in the 1840s.

SUMMER DROVING, *Arthur Streeton, 1891*

THE FRENCH IMPRESSIONISTS

Besides Claude Monet, leading Impressionists based in France included Frenchmen Edgar Degas (1834–1917), Edouard Manet (1832–83), Camille Pissarro (1830–1903) and Auguste Renoir (1841–1919), as well as American Mary Cassatt (1844–1926), Frenchwoman Berthe Morisot (1841–95) and Briton Alfred Sisley (1839–99).

MONET'S WATERLILIES
To explore the differing effects of light, Monet often painted the same subject over and over. In later life he worked in his studio, creating a series of vast canvases of the waterlily pond at his house at Giverny, near Paris.

SEURAT & POINTILLISM

One of the first spin-offs from Impressionism was a style usually known as Pointillism (from the French word *point* meaning 'dot') – although the artist who developed it in the 1880s, Frenchman Georges Seurat (1859–91), preferred to call it Divisionism.

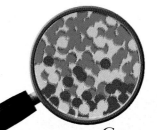

GOING DOTTY
Seurat's Pointilliste paintings are meant to be observed from a distance. Close up, you can see that they're composed of tiny dots of pure colour.

A SUNDAY AFTERNOON ON THE ISLAND OF LA GRANDE JATTE
GEORGES SEURAT, *c.* 1884–86

Seurat wanted to achieve something more permanent than a snapshot-like impression of what the eye sees in a glancing moment, and composed his paintings carefully to achieve order, balance and harmony.

This gave works such as *La Grande Jatte* a feeling of monumental stillness and calm. All this attention to detail took time, and Seurat worked on this particular painting in his studio for over a year.

8

SPOTS BEFORE THE EYES

The Impressionists had been greatly influenced by the latest scientific theories about colour and light, and their shimmering paintings tried to reproduce the way light appears to the eye when reflected off the surface of things. By the '80s, scientists had proved that light is picked up inside the eyeball as tiny coloured dots, which the brain then fuses into images – and this is what Seurat replicated with his new style.

UNMIXED PALETTE

To achieve the complementary colours green, purple and orange, the Impressionists had mixed the primary colours red, yellow and blue (blue and yellow make green, for example). Seurat aimed for even more vibrant colour effects by using dots of primary colour side by side – when he wanted a green, for example, he made it by painting thousands of tiny, separate, blue and yellow dots.

LAST WORDS
Seurat (above) died suddenly when he was 31. His friend and fellow Pointilliste Paul Signac (1863–1935) claimed he'd killed himself through overwork.

MODERN MONSTROSITY
Architects were also breaking with tradition. When the Eiffel Tower was completed in 1889, most people thought it an eyesore. Seurat, however, admired it and painted it the same year.

BLIND ALLEY
The Impressionist Camille Pissarro adopted Pointillism for a while in the '80s, but found it blocked his spontaneity.

VAN GOGH & GAUGUIN

Artists had gone about as far as they could in translating the science of light into the poetry of painting. A gradual shift away from naturalistic colour now went hand-in-hand with an increasing focus on emotions.

PERE TANGUY
VINCENT VAN GOGH, 1887

Van Gogh admired the expressive qualities of Japanese prints like the ones he copied in the background to this portrait. He also liked the strong, flat colours of Japanese prints, and the way that artists didn't try to reproduce exactly what was in front of their eyes.

WOODBLOCK PRINT by Kitagawa Utamaro (1753–1806), c. 1797

GOING JAPANESE

Japanese woodblock prints were first seen in Europe in the 1850s and had a profound influence on avant-garde Western art. The simplified forms, flat areas of colour, unusual composition and flattened perspective (sense of space and depth) were all new to Western eyes.

PAINTING FROM THE HEART

The Dutch painter Vincent van Gogh (1853–90) thought that although Impressionism could show what an artist saw, it couldn't portray feelings. By the end of his short life, he'd found a personal style of painting that expressed strong emotions such as joy, fear and sorrow.

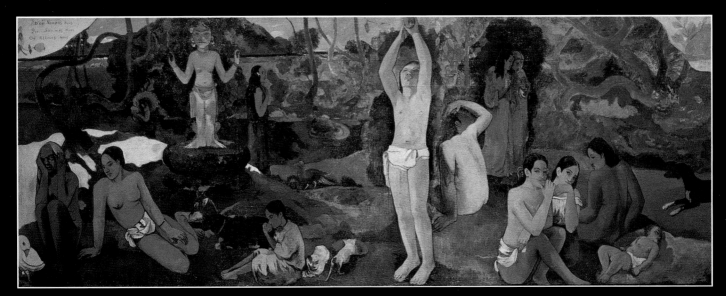

WHERE DO WE COME FROM? WHAT ARE WE? WHERE ARE WE GOING?
PAUL GAUGUIN, 1897

Turning his back on Western civilization, in '95 Gauguin moved to the South Pacific where he said he hoped to cultivate his art into 'something primitive and wild'.

He wanted to paint the inner world of the imagination and the soul. In *Where do we come from?*, he portrayed the cycle of life, from infancy (right) to old age (left).

AN ARTIST'S LIFE
Towards the end of his life, van Gogh was tormented by bouts of intense depression which drove him to suicide at the age of 37. Van Gogh's life has become as famous as his art, and he's been the subject of many books and films.

THE ART OF PASSION

Van Gogh used paint very thickly, laying it on the canvas with broad, passionate brushstrokes. Colours represented feelings – yellow, the colour of sunshine, evoked life, hope and happiness, for example. About one painting, *The Night Café* (1888), he said:

'I have tried to express the terrible passions of humanity by means of red and green.'

A PASSIONATE FRIENDSHIP

For a while van Gogh was friendly with the French artist Paul Gauguin (1848–1903) – it was after their friendship ended in a violent quarrel in '88 that van Gogh famously cut off his own earlobe. Van Gogh's paintings may look very different from his, but Gauguin was also developing a new, non-naturalistic style of painting.

In Lust for Life *(1956), van Gogh (left) was played by actor Kirk Douglas and Gauguin (right) by Anthony Quinn.*

MUNCH & EXPRESSIONISM

Although the style we call Expressionism didn't gather enough force to be labelled an art movement until the 1900s, its foundations were laid in the 1880s.

The artists who started the ball rolling were van Gogh and the Norwegian Edvard Munch (1863–1944), whose *The Scream* is one of the world's most famous paintings.

12

THE SCREAM
EDVARD MUNCH, 1893

Munch left us this description of the birth of his famous painting: 'I was tired and ill. I stood looking out across the fjord. The Sun was setting. The clouds were coloured red – like blood. I felt as though a scream went through nature…The colours were screaming.'

After having a nervous breakdown in 1908, Munch abandoned the anguished imagery of earlier work.

LETTING IT ALL HANG OUT

As its name suggests, Expressionism was all about expressing the artist's inner feelings. It was an anti-naturalistic style in which vigorous brushstrokes, and exaggerated or distorted shapes and colours, were used to cook up the biggest possible emotional storms. Unlike van Gogh, however, who created joyful paintings as well as sad ones, for many years Munch's artistic view of the world was like a long, waking nightmare.

WHERE'S MY MUMMY
One of Munch's inspirations for The Scream *was a mummified Inca that he saw at the Paris World's Fair in '89. For Munch, this mummy was the embodiment of fear and panic. Gauguin was also fascinated by it and used it as an image of death in some of his paintings.*

MIRROR OF THE SOUL

'For as long as I can remember I have suffered from a deep feeling of anxiety which I have tried to express in my art,' wrote Munch in a diary.

This wasn't surprising, given his tragic childhood – first his mother (in '68) and then his elder sister (in '77) died of tuberculosis, while his father, driven almost mad with grief, suffered from a religious mania that sometimes erupted into violence. Until his own breakdown in 1908, Munch's paintings were as tortured as his life. In them, he laid bare his innermost feelings, exploring the huge themes of love, sexual desire, sickness, death – and the howling fear and loneliness so vividly expressed in the swirling, unnatural colours and shapes of *The Scream*.

FREUDIAN ANALYSIS

By the '90s, Austrian psychoanalyst Sigmund Freud (1856–1939) was developing his theories on the workings of the human mind. He was to conclude that much of our behaviour is shaped by our unconscious, the part of our minds that contains memories, thoughts and feelings of which we are unaware. Although Freud's theories weren't widely known until well into the 20th century, painters such as Munch were already expressing them artistically in the 1890s.

Freud argued that dreams can contain clues to our unconscious.

13

SYMBOLISM

The 'isms' of art history are often invented by art critics well after the development of a new style, and can embrace artists whose work appears puzzlingly different. One of the most confusingly eclectic groupings of the late 19th century was Symbolism, an art movement that varied wildly in style and subject matter.

THE CYCLOPS, *Odilon Redon, 1898–1900*

Redon was described as the 'prince of mysterious dreams' by one critic. In Greek mythology, the one-eyed giant Cyclops was hopelessly in love with the nymph Galatea.

MATERIAL WORLD

Symbolism arose in reaction to the naturalism of Impressionism, and to the greedy materialism of modern industrial life. Gauguin was a leading Symbolist, and Munch is often described as one. Other Symbolists included Frenchmen Gustave Moreau (1826–98) and Odilon Redon (1840–1916), Dutchman Jan Toorop (1858–1928) and Austrian Gustav Klimt (1862–1918). Instead of depicting the real world, these artists drew upon their ideas, emotions, imaginations and dreams. Their subjects ranged from the exotic and the otherworldly, to the mystical and the erotic.

ARTISTIC LICENCE
Klimt was a big man with a huge appetite for life and for women. Much of his work was explicitly erotic and many of his contemporaries criticized it as corrupt and decadent.

ART NOUVEAU

In the decorative arts and architecture, the sinuous, curling line and stylized natural imagery of Art Nouveau were at the height of their popularity in the 1890s and early 1900s. The swirling shapes of some paintings of the period, including Munch's *The Scream* and Klimt's *The Kiss*, show the influence of Art Nouveau.

ART NOUVEAU lampshade by American Louis Comfort Tiffany (1848–1933)

14

THE KISS
GUSTAV KLIMT, 1907–08

A woman and a man kneel and kiss in a field of flowers, lost in their own golden dream of love. Klimt's work spanned Symbolism and Art Nouveau, and *The Kiss* is one of the world's most luxurious and decorative celebrations of sensuality.

Klimt had trained as an applied artist and he loved gold leaf and rich patterns. In the 1900s he created glittering mosaic murals for the Vienna Workshops, a group of artists and craftworkers who created the Austrian version of Art Nouveau.

FAUVISM

In 1905 the rumblings of an artistic revolution finally erupted into the first major avant-garde art movement of the 20th century – Fauvism.

THE WILD ONES

If art critics had rubbished the Impressionists back in the 1870s, it was nothing to what they said about the Fauves. Some described them as 'invertebrates' and 'incoherents', and when one critic – Louis Vauxcelles (*b.* 1870; *dod unknown*) – jokingly exclaimed that they painted like 'wild beasts' or *fauves*, the name stuck.

EXPLODING INTO COLOUR

What people found so shocking about the Fauves was their savagely unnatural use of colour. Henri Matisse (1869–1954) the group's leader, for example, painted a portrait of his wife with a bright green streak down the centre of her face.

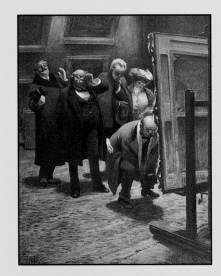

THE MASTERPIECE, *Albert Guillaume, 1905*

PICTURE PALACES
France's official annual art exhibition, the Paris Salon, dated from the 17th century and was a showcase for traditional painting and sculpture. People went there to admire conventional works of art – as shown left by an illustrator on the magazine *L'Illustration*. Founded in 1903, the Salon d'Automne was one of two major annual exhibitions set up in opposition to the Salon, to show modern art. The other was the Salon des Indépendants (formed in 1884).

THE POOL OF LONDON
ANDRÉ DERAIN, 1906

The outrage that met the Fauves' first exhibition was accompanied by instant fame in Parisian art circles, and several artists were offered contracts by art dealers. In late 1905 Derain was commissioned by the avant-garde dealer Ambroise Vollard (*c.* 1867–1939) to visit London, and he created some of his best Fauve works there. In *The Pool of London* as in other Fauve works, colour was the subject of the painting not the scene, which was transformed into a vibrating rainbow. 'Colours became charges of dynamite,' Derain wrote of Fauvism later... 'everything could be raised above the real.'

Where the Impressionists had used bright colours to represent natural light, the Fauves freed them from reality – their unnatural colours were bold and fierce, and often deliberately clashing.

SHORT BUT SWEET

All the Fauves were French, apart from Dutch-born Kees van Dongen (1877–1968). Besides Matisse, they included André Derain (1880–1954), Albert Marquet (1875–1947), Georges Rouault (1871–1958) and Maurice de Vlaminck (1876–1958). The group was rather short lived, though, and by 1907 they had gone their separate ways – some to continue exploring Fauvism on their own, others to experiment with new avant-garde styles.

PORTRAIT OF AMBROISE VOLLARD, *Paul Cézanne, 1899*

GOOD DEALER
Among the avant-garde painters championed by the art dealer Ambroise Vollard were Gauguin, van Gogh, Cézanne (1839–1906), Picasso, Matisse, Derain and de Vlaminck.

17

MATISSE, KING OF COLOUR

'What I am after above all is expression,' wrote Matisse in 1908... 'Expression to my way of thinking does not consist of the passion mirrored upon a human face... The whole arrangement of my pictures is expressive... Composition is the art of arranging in a decorative manner the various elements at a painter's disposal for the expression of his feelings.'

DEPTH OF COLOUR

Matisse was a genius who enriched art in all sorts of ways, from colour to composition. In traditional art, perspective is used to make paintings like mirrors, reflecting our eyes' three-dimensional view of the world around us. In works like *The Dance*, with its flat, blue and green background, Matisse helped shift the focus of composition from perspectival depth to the harmonious and expressive use of colour.

THE DANCE
HENRI MATISSE, 1910

With just three colours, Matisse expressed all the wild abandon of dancing. Although he created designs for the Russian Ballet in 1920, Matisse is supposed to have preferred country dancing and a circular, country dance called the *sardana* is said to have inspired *The Dance*. At 2.60 x 3.91 metres, it was commissioned as a huge mural for the Moscow house of Matisse's biggest patron, the Russian Sergei Shchukin (1854–1936).

The star of the Russian Ballet was Vaslav Nijinsky (1890–1950).

DANCING TO A NEW TUNE

A revolution took place in dance, too, in the 1900s. Believing the conventions of classical ballet to be artificial and meaningless, pioneers of modern dance such as the Russian Ballet explored freedom of expression and movement. The Russians caused a sensation when they first performed in Paris in 1909.

THE DOCTOR
As the oldest Fauve (36 in 1905), Matisse was their natural leader. His neat red beard made him look rather serious, and he was nicknamed the Doctor by younger friends.

18

MATISSE THE MASTER

Matisse was one of the great masters of 20th century art, and he went on experimenting throughout his long life. In his 70s, when illness left him bedridden, he began cutting out shapes from boldly painted sheets of paper. His assistants would then move the cut-outs about until he was satisfied with the colour balance and composition. Some of his most brilliant works, such as *The Snail* (1953), were created in this way, in the last years of his life.

FRIENDS IN NEED AND DEED
The experimental writer and art collector Gertrude Stein (1874-1946) was a friend and generous patron to Matisse and other avant-garde artists, including Picasso. Wealthy collectors played a crucial role in supporting modern artists early in their careers.

NORTHERN EXPRESSIONISM

The term Expressionism was first used in print in 1911, to describe a German avant-garde group founded in 1905, the year Paris was rocked by the first Fauve exhibition. Like the Fauves, the German artists distorted colour and shape. But where most of the Fauves' paintings radiated a kind of joyful harmony, those of the northern European Expressionists were generally far more jagged and nervy.

POSTER FOR MURDERER, HOPE OF WOMEN, *Oskar Kokoschka, 1909*

CITY CENTRES

The new German avant-garde group was founded in Dresden, a city on the banks of the River Elbe. But by 1911 the entire group had moved north to Berlin, where the artistic and social scene was far more vibrant – and decadent!

AUSTRIAN EXPRESSIONISTS

Other northern Europeans who explored Expressionism included the Austrians Egon Schiele (1890–1918) and Oskar Kokoschka (1886–1980). Kokoschka was a playwright as well as a painter, and made the poster above for one of his own plays.

20

BRIDGE OVER TROUBLED WATER

The Germans called themselves Die Brücke (German for 'the bridge') and the founder members were Fritz Bleyl (1880–1966), Erich Heckel (1883–1970), Ernst Ludwig Kirchner (1880–1938) and Karl Schmidt-Rottluff (1884–1976). One of Die Brücke's aims was to escape the dominance of French culture – 'We have a duty to separate ourselves from the French,' wrote Kirchner in 1912, a year before the group separated and went their own separate ways, 'it is time for an independent German art.'

SELF-PORTRAIT, *Paula Modersohn-Becker, 1900s*

WOMEN IN ART
Although little known at the time of her death, Paula Modersohn-Becker (1876–1907) was one of the leading German artists of the 1900s. It was still hard for women to train or be accepted as artists, particularly among the avant-garde. Even by the early 20th century, it was rare for women to be accepted into the best art schools – it was thought improper for them to make studies of nude models.

SELF-PORTRAIT WITH MODEL
ERNST LUDWIG KIRCHNER, 1910 (*overpainted in '26*)

The Die Brücke artists wanted to express themselves 'directly and passionately', and their main subject was their own way of life. Like many avant-garde artists of the period, they aimed for artistic and social freedom, leading bohemian lifestyles and deliberately flaunting accepted codes of social behaviour. Many of Kirchner's early paintings were set indoors in his studio, using himself and one of his many girlfriends as models. The model sitting on the bed in this portrait was called Dodo – she was the most important woman in Kirchner's art and life in 1909–11.

PICASSO'S *LES DEMOISELLES D'AVIGNON*

If traditional painting had held a mirror up to reality, in 1907 the Spanish artist Pablo Picasso (1881–1973) threw a stone at the mirror and shattered it. Even Picasso's friends were shocked by *Les Demoiselles d'Avignon* – one said that looking at it was like being made to drink petrol!

AFRICAN INSPIRATION

European colonization of Africa was at its height in the 19th century, and a flood of looted art objects appeared on the European art market. Few people in Europe, including Picasso, knew anything about the ritual or tribal meanings of this art, but they responded to its energy and freedom to distort reality.

A REVOLUTION IN ART

Picasso's painting was a guerrilla attack on the traditional treatment of form – the individual shapes in a work of art, and the relationships between them. Instead of a unified illusion of three-dimensional reality, he tried to compose his painting from angular two-dimensional planes, like bits of shattered glass.

22

TRIBAL MASK from the African Congo

STRANGE BEAUTY

The violently distorted, mask-like heads of the two women on the right of the painting were inspired by African masks – Picasso was enormously excited by seeing African sculptures at a Paris museum and said they were 'the most powerful and the most beautiful of all the products of the human imagination'. In the end Picasso was less happy with his painting, though, and *Les Demoiselles* was hidden away in a corner of his studio for years.

PORTRAIT OF THE ARTIST AS A YOUNG MAN
This photograph was taken in 1904, the year Picasso left Spain and settled in Paris.

LES DEMOISELLES D'AVIGNON
PABLO PICASSO, 1907

The viewpoints in Picasso's painting are deliberately confusing. Some of the women's eyes are painted front on, for example, but their noses are shown in profile, from the side. The head of the woman in the bottom right is fixed to her back, not her front.

Picasso also set out to shock people with his treatment of the painting's subject. In place of the soft and submissive female nudes of art history, he portrayed naked anger and aggression. Instead of celebrating beauty, he flaunted ugliness.

PAUL CEZANNE

Picasso's chief inspiration for the shifting viewpoints in *Les Demoiselles d'Avignon* came from the paintings of the great French artist Paul Cézanne (1839–1906).

THE HEART OF THE MATTER

Cézanne began painting in the 1860s, and although he experimented with Impressionism for a while, he soon decided that he wanted to do something more 'solid and durable'. The problem with Impressionism, Cézanne thought, was that it only dealt with the surface of nature. He wanted to get beneath its skin, to expose its heart and skeleton. In attempting to achieve this, he developed a new approach to volume – the space that a three-dimensional object appears to fill in a painting.

NO PLACE LIKE HOME
Cézanne was born in Aix-en-Provence in southern France, and studied law before moving to Paris to paint in his early 20s. In the 1880s he returned to Provence, remaining there until his death.

24

TRICKS OF THE TRADE
The techniques of perspective are used to give the illusion of three-dimensional space and depth on a flat surface. One technique is to draw lines that stretch into the distance, and which in real life are parallel, so that they meet on the horizon. Another is to make distant objects smaller than ones close by, even though in real life they are the same size.

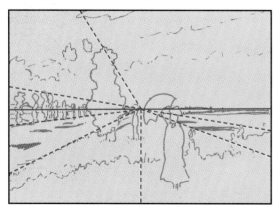

The place where perspective lines meet on the horizon is called the vanishing point.

A QUESTION OF PERSPECTIVE

Paintings are flat, two-dimensional objects, of course, and artists use perspective to give the illusion of space and depth. In traditional art, perspective was based on a single, fixed viewpoint. As Cézanne struggled to get to the heart of nature, however, he found it impossible to maintain this fixed viewpoint – whenever his eyes flickered or his head moved, his view shifted.

A CHANGE OF VIEWPOINT

Cézanne began to build this shifting viewpoint into later paintings, such as his scenes of Mont Sainte-Victoire. This is one reason why many people now consider him to be the greatest artist of the 19th century, and the most influential figure in the development of modern art – Picasso himself called Cézanne 'the father of us all'.

MONT SAINTE-VICTOIRE
PAUL CÉZANNE, 1904–05

Completed the year before he died, this is one of more than ten oil paintings in which Cézanne tried to capture the essence of a mountain near his home in Provence (*mont* is French for 'mountain'). There are no perspective devices leading our eyes towards the horizon in this landscape, as the trees do in Monet's *The Walk (Argenteuil)* on page 6. Instead both the mountain and the fields and trees in front of it seem near and faraway at the same time. Cézanne built his paintings from blocks of colour like the pieces in a mosaic, often showing things from different angles simultaneously.

25

ROOM WITH A VIEW
This photograph of Mont Sainte-Victoire was taken from the road outside Cézanne's studio.

CUBISM

Inspired by Cézanne's unique style of painting, and kickstarted by Picasso's outrageous *Les Demoiselles d'Avignon*, the revolutionary art movement known as Cubism exploded into life late in 1907. It was the joint creation of Picasso and his friend the French artist Georges Braque (1882–1963).

FAME AT LAST

Cézanne's work wasn't widely known until after 1895, when he was given a one-man show in Paris by the art dealer Ambroise Vollard. Among Cézanne's new admirers was the French artist Maurice Denis (1870–1943), who in 1890 had drawn attention to the contradictions of showing a three-dimensional scene on a two-dimensional surface. 'Remember,' Denis had declared, 'that a picture before being a war horse or a nude woman…is essentially a flat surface covered with colours assembled in a certain order.'

HOMAGE TO CÉZANNE, *Maurice Denis, 1900*

CAREER CHANGES
Braque lived into his 80s and his painting style changed at different stages of his career. In the '20s, he evolved a less angular, more fluid style than that of his early Cubist works.

CREATIVE PARTNERSHIP

Picasso and Braque worked together so closely over the next few years that it is often hard to tell their paintings apart – Braque said they were 'roped together like mountaineers'.

CRACKING THE PROBLEM

Together they achieved an entirely new way of looking at the world. The old idea of a single, fixed viewpoint was shattered, as Picasso and Braque finally succeeded in breaking apart people, objects and landscapes and painting them from several angles at once. The cube-like forms and geometric patterns that resulted gave rise to the term Cubism – coined by Louis Vauxcelles, the art critic who had named the Fauves back in 1905.

HOUSES AT L'ESTAQUE
GEORGES BRAQUE, 1908

Braque admired Cézanne hugely and in the summer of 1908 visited L'Estaque in southern France, where Cézanne had lived and worked in the 1870s.

In Braque's painting, the houses are triangles and cubes, like children's building bricks. Some of their corners seem to jut out of the canvas. Others point into it.

CONSTANTIN BRANCUSI

By the late 1900s, sculpture, like painting, stood poised between the old world and the new. The most radical sculptor of the period, and one of the most respected and influential of all 20th-century artists, was Constantin Brancusi (1876–1957). Although born in Romania, Brancusi settled in France in 1904.

GRAND OLD MAN OF ART
By 1900 Rodin was so well-respected that an entire pavilion was devoted to his sculptures at the World's Fair in Paris.

ACORN OF INDEPENDENCE

In Paris, Brancusi met the great French sculptor Auguste Rodin (1840–1917), whom he admired enormously and whose influence showed in his work. When Rodin offered to take him on as an assistant, though, Brancusi refused. 'No other tree,' he said, 'can grow in the shadow of an oak.'

THE ART OF SCULPTURE, THE MEANING OF A KISS

By 1907, Brancusi was beginning to develop his own distinctive style, based on the simplification of form to create universal truths – things so powerful that they speak to our deepest feelings. He called his first sculpture in this new style *The Kiss* and created it in about 1908. It has the same title as Rodin's famous sculpture, but the two works are centuries apart.

CARVED IN STONE
Brancusi was a master stonecarver and helped bring about a revival of direct carving – making a sculpture by cutting directly into the material. In the 19th century, sculptors modelled their work in clay or wax. It was expensive to have something cast in bronze or carved in marble, so usually this was done only after a sculpture was paid for. Successful sculptors such as Rodin employed assistants to copy their work in stone, sometimes adding the finishing touches.

THE KISS,
*Auguste
Rodin, 1886*

28

THE KISS
CONSTANTIN BRANCUSI, *c.* 1908

Carved from a single block of stone, two lovers are locked in their kiss for eternity. Brancusi said that his distinctive style was based on his feeling that: 'what is real is not the external form but the essence of things. Starting from this truth it is impossible for anyone to express anything essentially real by imitating its exterior surface.' He made a series of versions of *The Kiss* and one, carved in 1909, was installed in the Parisian cemetery of Montparnasse on the grave of a young girl who had committed suicide.

FLIGHT OF FANCY
One of Brancusi's bird sculptures is towards the back of this photograph of his studio. 'Why write [about my sculptures],' he once said. 'Why not just show the photographs?'

THE SIMPLE LIFE

Brancusi carried on refining and simplifying his sculpture throughout his long life. His themes of creation, life and death were monumental, but his subjects were as pared down as his style – heads purified into egg shapes that symbolize dreaming and creation, and birds elongated into teardrops that soar upwards through space and time.

29

GLOSSARY

ART NOUVEAU A decorative style of the 1880s–1900s, characterized by stylized plant and animal motifs and sinuous, curling patterns.

AVANT-GARDE In art, someone who pioneers a new and experimental style or technique.

COMPOSITION The way the elements of a work of art, such as shape, are combined into a satisfactory whole.

CUBISM An art style born in 1907 which overthrew the 500-year-old tradition in Western painting of a single, fixed viewpoint. In Cubism, the subject is fragmented into geometric shapes and several viewpoints are presented at once.

EXPRESSIONISM An art style that originated in the 1880s and flourished from 1905 onwards. Expressionist artists sought to express emotion through exaggerated or distorted colours and shapes.

FAUVISM An exuberant French form of Expressionism which flowered in the mid-1900s.

FORM The individual shapes in a work of art, and the relationships between them.

IMPRESSIONISM A style that originated in the late 1860s, in which artists aimed for spontaneous impressions of everyday scenes, and tried to capture the fleeting effects of light reflecting off the surface of things.

PERSPECTIVE The illusion of three-dimensional space and depth created on a flat, two-dimensional surface such as an artist's canvas.

POINTILLISM An art style in which colour tones were suggested by using dots of pure, unmixed colour. It developed in the 1880s.

SYMBOLISM An influential movement in literature and the visual arts, which flourished in the 1880s–1900s. It emphasized the world of imagination, emotion, dreams and ideas.

VIENNA WORKSHOPS An association of artists and craftworkers founded in Austria in 1903 to promote the manufacture of high-quality, handcrafted goods.

VOLUME The space that a three-dimensional object appears to fill in a painting. Also known as mass.

WORLD EVENTS

- China: Boxer Rising against foreigners
- Britain: formation of Labour Party
- Commonwealth of Australia proclaimed
- Britain: death of Queen Victoria
- South Africa: second Boer War ends
- Signing of Anglo-Japanese Alliance
- Wright brothers achieve first powered flight
- Britain: Women's Social & Political Union formed
- Japan & Russia at war (to '05)
- Entente Cordiale (Britain & France)
- Norway independent (of Sweden)
- First revolution in Russia
- USA: hundreds die in San Francisco earthquake
- End of Dreyfus Affair in France – Dreyfus cleared
- New Zealand gets Dominion status
- Triple Entente (Russia, France & Britain)
- Austria annexes Bosnia-Herzegovina
- Henry Ford launches Model T car
- Blériot makes first flight across Channel
- Peary & Henson reach North Pole

19
19
19
19
19
19
19
19
19
19
19
19
19

TIMELINE

	ART	DESIGN	THEATRE & FILM	BOOKS & MUSIC
00	•Art & sculpture of 29 nations exhibited at Paris World's Fair •Redon: The Cyclops	•Art Nouveau celebrated at Paris World's Fair •H. Guimard designing Art Nouveau Paris Métro	•Henrik Ibsen: When We Dead Awaken •Box Brownie camera launched	•Sigmund Freud: The Interpretation of Dreams •Giacomo Puccini: Tosca
01	•Start of Picasso's Blue Period (to 1904) •Small Cézanne show at Vollard's Paris gallery	•V. Horta's Art Nouveau A L'Innovation department store in Brussels	•Anton Chekhov: The Three Sisters •Strindberg: Dance of Death	•Rudyard Kipling: Kim •E. Elgar's march Pomp and Circumstance (No. 1)
02		•C.R. Mackintosh's Willow Tea Rooms, Glasgow (to '04) •D.H. Burnham's Flatiron Building, New York	•First science fiction film: George Méliès' 14-minute A Trip to the Moon	•Scott Joplin's ragtime tune 'The Entertainer' •Conan Doyle: The Hound of the Baskervilles
03	•Deaths of Gauguin & Pissarro •Paris: Salon d'Automne founded, for modern art	•Vienna Workshops (arts & crafts association) founded	•First western film: Edwin S. Porter's 11-minute The Great Train Robbery	•Jack London: Call of the Wild •Henry James: The Ambassadors
04	•Picasso moves to Paris & sets up home there •Matisse's Luxe, Calme et Volupté ignites Fauvism	•Otto Wagner's modernist Post Office Savings Bank, Vienna (to '06)	•J.M. Barrie: Peter Pan •Abbey Theatre opens, in Dublin	•Giacomo Puccini: Madame Butterfly •Joseph Conrad: Nostromo
05	•Paris: first Fauve exhibition causes uproar •Dresden: Die Brücke founded (Expressionism)	•Barcelona: Antonio Gaudí's Art Nouveau Casa Milá (to '07) & Casa Battló (to '17)	•G.B. Shaw: Mrs Warren's Profession •First nickelodeon film theatres open in USA	•Albert Einstein: Special Theory of Relativity •Franz Lehár: The Merry Widow
06	•Derain's Fauve The Pool of London •Death of Cézanne	•McKim, Mead & White's classical style Pennsylvania Station, NY (to '10)	•C. Tait's 80-minute film, The Story of the Kelly Gang •One of first cartoon films made, by J. Stuart Blackton	•John Galsworthy's first Forsythe Saga novel: The Man of Property
07	•Klimt: The Kiss (to '08) •Picasso's Les Demoiselles d'Avignon sparks off birth of Cubism	•Deutsche Werkbund (arts, crafts & industry association) founded in Munich	•J.M. Synge: The Playboy of the Western World •Ziegfeld Follies opens in New York	•Hillaire Belloc: Cautionary Tales •Maxim Gorky: Mother
08	•Braque's Cubist Houses at L'Estaque •Brancusi's early versions of The Kiss	•Peter Behrens' modernist AEG Turbine Factory, Berlin (to '09)		•E.M. Forster: A Room With a View •Kenneth Grahame: The Wind in the Willows
09	•Publication of Italian writer F.T. Marinetti's first Futurist manifesto, in French paper Le Figaro	•Frank Lloyd Wright's Prairie-style Robie House, Chicago	•Russian Ballet first performs in Paris •Pathé newsreel introduced in France	•Gustav Mahler: The Song of the Earth •Rabindranath Tagore: Gitanjali (Song Offerings)

INDEX

African art 22
architecture 9, 14
art critic 5, 16, 26
art dealer 16, 17, 26
Art Nouveau 14, 15, 30
art patron 18, 19
avant-garde 30

Berlin 20
Bleyl, Fritz 21
Brancusi, Constantin 28–29
Braque, Georges 26–27
Brücke, Die 20–21

Cassatt, Mary 7
Cézanne, Paul 17, 24–25, 26, 27
complementary colour 7, 9
composition 10, 18, 30
Cubism 26–27, 30
Cyclops, The (Redon) 14

dance, modern 18
Dance, The (Matisse) 18–19
Degas, Edgar 7
Demoiselles d'Avignon, Les (Picasso) 22–23, 24, 26
Denis, Maurice 26
Derain, André 16, 17
direct carving 28
Divisionism, see Pointillism
Dresden 20
Douglas, Kirk 11

Eiffel Tower 9
Expressionism 12–13, 20–21, 30

Fauvism 16–17, 18, 20, 26, 30

form 22, 30
Freud, Sigmund 13

Gare Saint-Lazare, La (Monet) 5
Gauguin, Paul 11, 13, 14, 17
Guillaume, Albert 16

Heckel, Erich 21
Homage to Cézanne (Denis) 26
Houses at L'Estaque (Braque) 27

Impressionism 5, 6–7, 8, 9, 10, 14, 16, 17, 24, 30
Incas 13
invention 7

Japanese art 10

Kirchner, Ernst Ludwig 21
Kiss, The (Brancusi) 28, 29
Kiss, The (Klimt) 14, 15
Kiss, The (Rodin) 28
Klimt, Gustav 14, 15
Kokoschka, Oskar 20

Lust for Life (film) 11

Manet, Edouard 7
Marquet, Albert 17
Matisse, Henri 16, 17, 18–19
Modersohn-Becker, Paula 21
Monet, Claude 5, 6, 7, 25
Mont Sainte-Victoire (Cézanne) 25
Moreau, Gustave 14
Morisot, Berthe 7

Munch, Edvard 12–13, 14
Murderer, Hope of Women (Kokoschka) 20

Night Café, The (van Gogh) 11
Nijinsky, Vaslav 18

optics, science of 7, 9, 11

paint tube, metal 7
Paris 4, 5, 7, 16, 22, 28
Père Tanguy (van Gogh) 10
perspective 5, 10, 18, 24, 25, 30
photography 6
Picasso, Pablo 4, 17, 19, 22–23, 24, 25, 26
Pissarro, Camille 7, 9
Pointillism 8–9, 30
Pool of London, The (Derain) 16–17
Portrait of Ambroise Vollard (Cézanne) 17
primary colour 7, 9
psychoanalysis 13

Redon, Odilon 14
Renoir, Auguste 7
Roberts, Tom 7
Rodin, Auguste 28
Rouault, Georges 17
Russian Ballet, the 18

Salon, the 16
Salon d'Automne 16
Salon des Indépendants 16
Schiele, Egon 20
Schmidt-Rottluff, Karl 21
science 7, 9, 10
Scream, The (Munch) 12, 13, 14

sculpture 28–29
Self-Portrait (Modersohn-Becker) 21
Self-Portrait with Model (Kirchner) 21
Seurat, Georges 8–9
Shchukin, Sergei 18
Signac, Paul 9
Sisley, Alfred 7
Snail, The (Matisse) 19
Stein, Gertrude 19
stonecarving 28
Streeton, Arthur 7
Summer Droving (Streeton) 7
Sunday Afternoon on the Island of La Grande Jatte, A (Seurat) 8
Symbolism 14–15, 30

technology 5
Tiffany, Louis Comfort 14
Toorop, Jan 14

Utamaro, Kitagawa 10

van Dongen, Kees 17
van Gogh, Vincent 10–11, 12, 13, 17
vanishing point 24
Vauxcelles, Louis 16, 26
Vlaminck, Maurice de 17
Vollard, Ambroise 16, 17, 26
volume 24, 30
Vienna Workshops 15, 30

Walk (Argenteuil), The (Monet) 6–7, 25
Where Do We Come From? (Gauguin) 11
women 7, 21
World's Fair, Paris 4, 5, 13, 28